METROPOLITAN
POLICE IMAGES

Motor Vehicles

A traffic officer directing traffic at Elephant and Castle in 1970.

Metropolitan Police Images

Motor Vehicles

*Michael R. Arden, Eleanor Fletcher
and Christopher Taylor*

PHILLIMORE

2008
Published by
PHILLIMORE & CO. LTD
Chichester, West Sussex, England
www.phillimore.co.uk
www.thehistorypress.co.uk

ISBN 978-1-86077-501-7

Printed and bound in Great Britain

Contents

List of Illustrations

Acknowledgements

The authors would like to thank the following individuals: Maggie Bird, Andy Bundle and Alastair Thompson for their help, expertise and advice. In particular we would like to thank Simon Littlejohn for his great effort in cataloguing, numbering and filing a mass of photographs: without this work it would have been impossible to tackle the project.

Introduction

Police vehicles are another of those clues, like particular songs, that can instantly set your mind back to a particular time or place. The older amongst us will probably remember the evocative opening clip from the 1960s TV series 'No Hiding Place' in which a black Wolseley patrol car roars out on to London's Embankment, warning bells ringing, from what is now Parliament's Norman Shaw Building but what was then New Scotland Yard. Similarly, the Ford Granada became an icon of the Seventies largely as a result of its role as an unmarked police car in 'The Sweeney'.

The primary purposes of police vehicles have always been to transport police officers to allow them to respond to the public's request for assistance and to apprehend those that break the law. Of course, there are many other functions covered within these broad categories including the transport of prisoners, provision of command and control, surveillance, patrol and many other specialist roles. Today's police car not only has warning lights and sirens but secure digital communication links, TV cameras, automated car recognition technology and real time remote access to several crime recording computer databases. Its carbon footprint is also likely to be a more important selection criterion than its 0-60 acceleration time.

This book brings together a sample of photographs of police vehicles drawn from the Metropolitan Police Service's Historic Collections. It covers the wide range of conveyances from a time nearer to our birth in 1829 right up to the present time. I hope this snapshot of the Met's vehicles will entertain and amuse you.

Stuart Middleton
Director of Transport Services
Metropolitan Police Service

Prison Vans

1 1881 engraving of Bow Street Magistrates' Court and Police Station. The image features a horse-drawn prison van. All prison vans were originally based at the Met's base in Nine Elms, before moving to Lambeth where the Met's fleet is based today.

2 An 1880s engraving of a prison van taking prisoners away from Bow Street Magistrates' Court. The basic design of the prison van has not changed to this day: each prisoner has a cell with an air vent or window each. This horse-drawn wagon would have carried up to twelve prisoners.

3 1897 photograph of a 'Black Maria' or prison van. The officer with feathers in his helmet is an Assistant Commissioner.

4 This photograph is dated about 1904 and was taken outside the old South Western Magistrates' Court, Lavender Hill. The image shows a civilian driver who is dressed in the new uniform which was introduced in 1904 following a complaint by the Commissioner that the drivers were untidy in their dress. This is an early example of outsourcing as both drivers and horses were provided by Thomas Tillings and operated from two main stables in Kings Cross and Old Kent Road.

5   1934 prison van, Leyland Cub with Marshalls of Cambridge bodywork. This van has twelve cells. The design and look of prison vans was starting to standardise at this date.

6   1938 Leyland prison van with bespoke bodywork. The photograph is taken at Nine Elms and features a despatch van in the background.

7 & 8 Prison van in Hyde Park in 1951. The vehicle is a (GR) Bedford OB. These were the first prison vans with escape hatches on the roof which allowed prisoners to evade death in crashed vehicles that were on fire. Same basic design as today's prison van. The van has fourteen cells, seven each side.

9   Prison van from1953, a Bedford S Type chassis with Maxeta bodywork. This particular model was utilised by the Met, right up until the mid-1980s.

10   Another Bedford S Type chassis with Maxeta bodywork in 1963.

11   1969 prison van, Bedford TK with customised bodywork by GC Smith. This photograph is taken at the Peel Centre in Hendon, on the athletics track. This is a twelve-cell van with escape hatches along the top.

12   1983 Prison van: Bedford Bus chassis, with Locomotors bodywork. This vehicle had fourteen prison cells. The original prison vans were dark blue (see earlier pictures) but this is one of the new white and stripe liveried vehicles that the Met adopted, known initially as the 'jam sandwich'.

Police Vans

13 1908 photograph of Met despatch vans and drivers. The small vehicles are six horse-power Siddeleys (the company that went on to become famous for aeroplane manufacture). The larger vehicles are ten horse-power Adam-Hewitts (made in Essex). The despatch service still exists to this day and plays an integral part in transferring correspondence and other items around the Metropolitan Police District.

14 This is a despatch van with civilian staff. The photograph is taken outside Bow Street Magistrates' Court.

15   First image from a set of demonstration photographs *c*.1931, showing officers being deployed in a station van. The van is a Leyland, with bodywork by Marshalls of Cambridge. The driver is identifiable by his flat hat (only drivers were issued flat hats until the early 1970s). This image shows the office taking the call. The job of station van driver was much sought after: once a driver, you would await calls in the station all day. Unlike today, a van never went out without a call. It usually took at least fifteen years of service to become a van driver.

16 Second image from a set of demonstration photographs showing officers being deployed in a station van. This image shows three officers rushing for the van (note that the driver is on the wrong side!).

17   Third image from a set of demonstration photographs showing officers being deployed in a station van. This image shows the officers speaking to a witness next to a Police Box.

18 1928/9 Morris Commercial station van. The driver is a member of police staff. This is the Divisional station van, there was one per Division. Calls would arrive from the call box and be allocated to the Drivers' Room in the Police Station where the driver would wait.

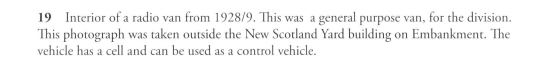

19 Interior of a radio van from 1928/9. This was a general purpose van, for the division. This photograph was taken outside the New Scotland Yard building on Embankment. The vehicle has a cell and can be used as a control vehicle.

20 & 21 This is a despatch van as can be seen from the civilian driver and attendant. The vehicle is an early 1930s Morris Commercial.

22 This is another general purpose, Ford A van. In the background can also be seen a Ford Model A car, and a Ford V8 pilot. This photograph was taken in the Kensal Rise railyard.

23 This is a general purpose van, a Model A Ford Truck in 1932. The bodywork is bespoke.

24 This is a radio truck from the late 1950s. The vehicle is an AEC and was built in Southall, west London. The truck is fitted with a ring aerial around the roof, which is unusual on a vehicle as they were designed for trains. This radio truck would form part of the mobile column which would be mobilised in the event of a nuclear attack. The vehicle would also have been used at large public order events, such as Wembley football matches. The radio trucks were parked at the old New Scotland Yard on Embankment.

25 This is the interior of a Morris LD station van in the late 1950s. Until the mid-1980s, all station vans were equipped with a ramp and winch so that motorcycles could be picked up and impounded. The same basic layout has continued to the present day: there were never double seats in the station van so that the passenger could easily pass into the back in case of trouble. The officer pictured is an Acting Sergeant; this is denoted by the two stripes on his sleeve.

26 1950s Austin station van or prison van with a Ford Anglia next to it and a Rover P3 in the background. This picture was taken by the windmill on Wimbledon Common in 1960.

27 The buses are Bedford TK with Maxeta bodywork. The picture was taken in 1965 and the control vehicle in front of the buses is a Morris LD, a pre-1963 model. The car is a Wolseley 6-90, a brand new area car. The photograph is taken just inside Hyde Park, behind Apsley House (No. 1 London) and the officers are attending a public order event. It was only in 1978 that riot wear was brought in for public order work.

28   This photograph shows communications equipment in a Bedford RL lorry with a canvas top. These vehicles were to be used as mobile columns in the event of a nuclear attack at the height of the Cold War. The photograph was taken around 1965.

29   A glimpse inside a Morris LD control van at Epsom Downs Racecourse which was then part of the Metropolitan Police District. Note the vehicle's cupola which indicates that it was operated by the Information Room at New Scotland Yard. These vehicles were often used to police protest marches, hence the cupola. The van would be driven slowly at the front of a march and officers would use the cupola to scan the crowd for signs of trouble.

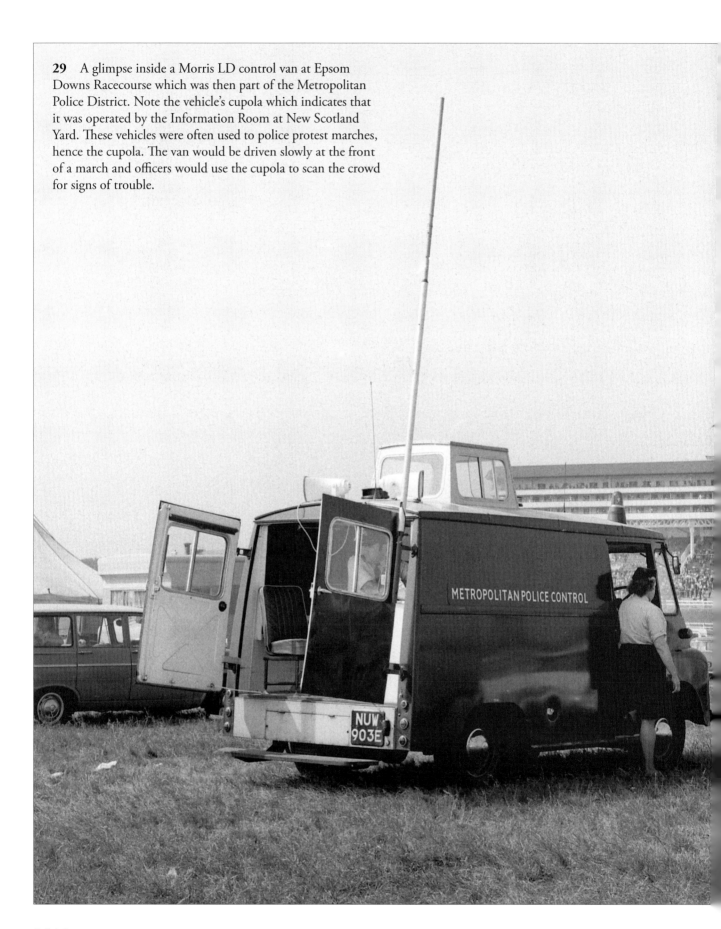

30 The vehicle in front is a 1964 Morris LD van, followed by a 1967 Austin J4. The photograph was taken at Wanstead and features towing training.

31 A Morris J3 police van. The officers have stopped a Ford Anglia van.

32-6 This is a 1973 Bedford KM 'Z Wagon': so called because of the shape of the lifting equipment, which was built by Telehoist. The 'Z Wagon' is lifting a CID car, the 1970 Hillman Hunter. The individual in the plain uniform is a police staff vehicle removal officer. These photographs were taken in 1973 at Nine Elms in South London.

37 Ford Transit Mark 1, 1974. This was an accident investigation vehicle used by traffic officers following a serious road traffic accident.

38 A 1977 Ford Transit 180 2.0L Special Patrol Group Carrier. This unit was formed in 1962 and disbanded in 1986, upon the establishment of the Territorial Support Group which continues to perform a similar function today. These vans were extremely unpopular with a large part of London's population and the mere appearance of this vehicle could trigger trouble.

39 This is a Morris Marina van, used by SOCOs (Scene of Crime Officers) in 1979. Behind is an Austin Allegro panda car and a Mini van (also used by SOCOs).

40   A 1987 photograph of a Leyland Sherpa 200. This was taken on the A40 outside Paddington Green Police Station. The A40 was closed at the time for repaving and the Metropolitan Police seized the opportunity to use the road for a multiple crash exercise.

41 & 42 1987 Freight Rover Sherpa 400 3.5 V-8. This is the original Territorial Support Group van. Normally this would carry six personnel, as, if they were overloaded with ten officers, the brakes would not function correctly. The grilles are locked up in place so an officer had to actually leave the van in order to lower them safely (otherwise the windscreen would crack).

43 A 1989 Vauxhall Astramax 1.6L van. This is an Accident Investigation Unit, based at Hampton Traffic Garage. Each of the traffic garages had one of these, and the vehicle carries with it all the necessary kit including the skid test, laptop, measuring equipment as well as apparatus which tests road conditions.

44 1995 LDV Sherpa 200 ½ tonne van. The Sherpa was the most common area van, in service from 1974 onwards. A design fault led to the doors falling off with some frequency!

45   1995 LDV Sherpa 400 3.9Efi V-8 with MacNeillie Armoured Bodywork. This is a
Territorial Support Group personnel carrier.

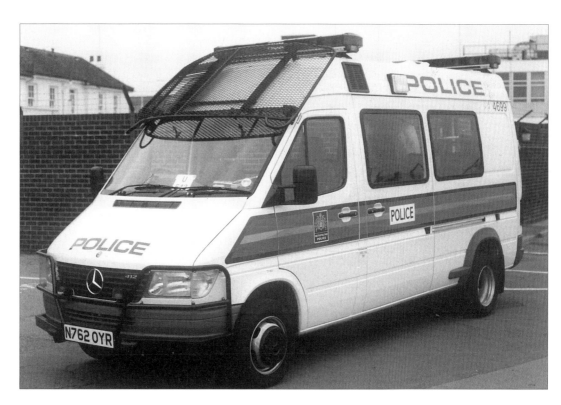

46   1996 Mercedes Benz Sprinter 412D, this vehicle was specially designed for the MPS and is
known as the 'Sprinter Met Spec'. The armoured conversion was done by Bedwas. These vehicles are
still in use for Territorial Support Group. Now all forces use this model, following the Met's lead.

47 1996 Volkswagen Transporter Type IV 2.0i with MacReady Conversion. This was another incarnation of the station van.

48 2001 Ford Transit 120 2.5Tdi. This is the standard station van and divisional prisoner transporter.

Motorcycles

49   This is a BSA (British Small Arms) motorcycle in the late 1930s. The photograph was taken at the Peel Centre and marks a graduating class for traffic officers.

50 These are BSA (British Small Arms) motorcycles in *c*.1965. This is the Metropolitan Police Motorcycle Display Team which was transformed into the Special Escort Group. The SEG exists today and contains the elite motorcyclists of the Met; it is deployed in escorting VIP cars and cavalcades.

51   This is a Triumph Angel motorcycle *c*.1965.

52 One of the earliest Triumph 650s, in 1968. This is one of the first motorcycle models to feature fairing at the front.

53 This motorcycle is a 1963 Triumph 750. This photograph shows a basic motorcycle training course, being run at Wanstead. The picture was taken *c.*1968.

54 & 55   These photographs were taken in 1968 and show an officer riding a Triumph motorcycle.

56 Triumph motorcycle.

57 This is a police motorcyclist in the late 1960s. The officer is dismounted and has stopped a Morris van.

58 & 59 These images show a traffic officer directing traffic at Elephant and Castle. The images are from 1970.

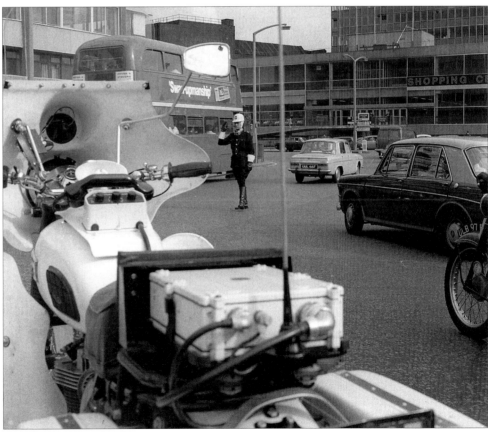

60 This is a traffic officer on a Triumph motorcycle. The tax disc displays the date May 1970 which means the photograph was taken in the twelve months preceding that date.

61 Special Escort Group officer on a Triumph motorcycle at Hyde Park Corner in 1970.

62   This is the Motorcycle Display Team at a Police Open Day.

63 This is the Motorcycle Display Team at a Police Open Day.

64-8 This is the Motorcycle Display Team at a Police Open Day.

69   This is a traffic sergeant from the Royal Parks Constabulary. The RPC were set up in 1872 to police London's eight Royal Parks. They were incorporated into the Met in 2004. The motorcycle is a Triumph.

70 Police motorcyclist on a Triumph in 1971. This photograph was taken around the Tulse Hill area.

71 & 72 This is a BMW Boxer 600 with Avon fairing in 1978. The publicity photographs show a police motorcyclist posing at Vauxhall, South London. This bike was on evaluation and was not adopted.

73-5 This is a Metropolitan Police motorcyclist, followed by a despatch van. The bike is a BMW 600 Boxer with Avon fairing. Photograph 1978, taken on the Walworth Road in south-east London.

76-8 Special Escort Group outside New Scotland Yard. The motorcycle is a BMW 800 Boxer without a fairing, 1979.

79 & 80   These are 1997 BMW R100s which were custom built for the Special Escort Group. These motorcycles were ordered in a hurry to be deployed at Princess Diana's funeral.

81   These are 1997 BMW R100 which were custom built for the Special Escort Group.

Cars

82   This is a Crossley Buggy Car from 1901/2. It is possible that this was the first car the Metropolitan Police owned. Certainly, the registration A209 was the first the Met ever owned. This car would have been used by the Commissioner to travel around the Metropolitan Police District.

83 This shows a row of Crossleys and Jowetts pictured outside a garage in Banbury, Oxfordshire. All but one of the vehicles is for the Metropolitan Police and has been issued with London County Council registrations starting 'YF'. The car with registration starting 'UD' is probably the garage's own demonstration model. One car carries the index UD 682,

an Oxfordshire number issued between May 1926 and discontinued in January 1929. The 'Metropolitan Police' cars all carry a YF registration, a London County Council index mark which was not issued after 1929. So the picture was obviously taken in Banbury between May 1926 and January 1929.

84 This is a line-up photograph of the Traffic Division at Croydon Traffic Garage. The photograph was taken in about 1930. This garage was opened in 1926 and is still used by the Metropolitan Police Service today.

85 This a Bentley 4.5 litre Flying Squad car *c.*1930/1. The Flying Squad was set up in 1919 in response to a crime wave that followed the First World War. The name derives from the fact that the original cars formerly belonged to the Royal Flying Corps. Flying Squad officers were specially trained in fast driving and this branch often had the most advanced vehicles in the MPS.

86   Three-wheeler vehicle, BSA (British Small Arms), *c.*1931.

87   Wolseley Series II, photographed at the Police Training College in Hendon, north-west London. This is a vehicle inspection, August 1937.

88 This is a Flying Squad Bentley in *c*.1936/7. This picture was taken on the North Circular road which had recently opened.

89 This is a Traffic exercise at the Regency Street Training Centre. All the officers are in flat caps, which denotes their driver status. This picture was taken in the late 1930s, and features an Austin 7 and a BSA (British Small Arms) traffic motorcycle combination. The officer on the left is an Inspector, as you can tell from the pips on his collar. This high collar uniform was standard issue up until 1962.

90 This photograph was taken outside the original New Scotland Yard (a red-brick Norman Shaw building on Embankment). The vehicle is a Ford traffic car – these were the only vehicles equipped with the 'Stop Police' sign. This sign dropped down on a pull cord: officers could release it once they had pulled in front of a vehicle they wished to pull over. The officer is from B District (Kensington, Chelsea & Notting Hill) on Point Duty in the Embankment area.

91   These traffic patrol cars are 1933 14.9 horse-power Tudor Saloon Fords. The photograph is taken outside the original New Scotland Yard on Embankment. The vehicles in the background are despatch vans.

92 This is a photograph of a Public Address car (see the address system on the roof). This car is deployed on crowd control outside the House of Commons, on the occasion of the abdication of Edward VIII in 1936. The PA car was staffed by a PA officer plus a radio operator; this was one of the cars equipped with a Morse Code machine in the late 1930s. The vehicle is a 1935 Wolseley.

93 Interior of a Flying Squad car, featuring a detective using one of the all-new Pye radio sets. The photograph was taken in the early 1950s and features a member of the Finchley Flying Squad, who covered north London.

94 A staged photograph of forensics training. The vehicle is a 1950 Standard Vanguard.

95 1956/7 Vauxhall Ventura. This photograph was taken at the Training School at the Peel Centre in Hendon. The instructing officer is a Station Sergeant as he has a crown above the usual three sergeant's stripes. Individuals in this position often had more power than those several ranks above as they controlled the whole workings of the police station.

96 This is a photograph of a 1957 Austin A95 Westminster. This vehicle is from the Driver Training School fleet.

97 Traffic car, a Wolseley 6/80, fitted with a Winkworth bell and speakers on the roof. The officer is a Traffic PC as you can tell by the T on his shoulder, plus the fact that his hat is a little squashed (Traffic Officers pushed their hats into their pockets when not wearing them). Photograph *c.*1959.

98 1956 Wolseley traffic car. This car carries a registration of 'BLL' which is the origin of the term 'Old Bill' as the Metropolitan Police had a whole series of these registrations on many vehicles.

99 This is a training exercise at the Peel Centre Training School in Hendon, dealing with a minor personal injury collision. The officers all have the Training School shoulder initials. The picture dates from the early 1960s, as all the badges are blacked out. The car is an Austin.

100 This is a Mini Cooper in 1968. This was deployed for traffic patrols on the A3 in south-west London. It was based at Surbiton Traffic Garage. This was the only Mini Cooper ever deployed.

101 Traffic officers directing traffic on the A4 by Osterley Underground station in 1968.

102 This is a traffic Land Rover Series 2. This 109-inch van worked on the M1 motorway. This photograph was taken in 1965 and shows the vehicle liveried with a non-reflective stripe which was an experiment in that year. The photograph also shows the equipment that it carried.

103 1969 Land Rover Series 2, towing a Ford Escort. This vehicle is equipped with a dot matrix sign.

104 1965 Austin Cambridge, photographed at the now obsolete Wanstead training centre. The photograph is taken in the late 1960s and is unusual as it features a WPC undergoing a five-week course to learn to drive. At this time, it was very rare for female officers to be booked onto any kind of driving course.

105 This Daimler Dart SP250 is a traffic car in 1964.

106   This is a 1960 Wolseley 6-90, pictured on the Hendon skid pan, taken in 1968 (the original is a rare colour photograph for this date). The building in the background is the old Driver Training School, long since demolished and replaced. You can tell from the patch at the front of the roof, that this was an old area car. The cars parked in the background include a Jaguar and a Rover P6, Mark 1.

107 This is a 1967 Jaguar traffic car and looks brand new. The tax disc expires in May 1968.

108 & 109 This is a Mark 2 Jaguar, with a 1970 Triumph 650 alongside. These photographs are taken outside County Hall, on the south bank of the River Thames.

110 & 111   This is the 1971 Land Rover Series 3, 109-inch van. The vehicle is fitted with a dot matrix sign across the roof. This was for use on motorways but the computer which operated the sign filled all the space in the back of this vehicle.

112 This is a Rover P6 on the A3 at New Malden in 1971.

113 Rover 3500 P6, Mark 2 on the A40 by the Hoover building in 1971. The van on the other side of the road is a Metropolitan Police Austin J4 despatch van.

114 Rover P6 Mark 2 on Muswell Hill in 1971.

115 This is a night photograph of a Rover P6 traffic car in 1971.

116-18   This is the Rover 3500 P6, mark 1. These images show the Rover being deployed as a traffic car engaged on a routine patrol in south-west London in 1971.

119-22 This is the Queen's Rolls Royce being escorted by the Special Escort Group (formerly the Motorcycle Display Team), riding Triumph 650s. The Queen's vehicle is being followed by a police armour-plated Rover 3500 P6 Mark 2. In some of the photographs you can also see a police Daimler Royale bringing up the rear. The photographs are taken as the cavalcade drives down Horse Guards Road, and past the Foreign and Commonwealth Office.

123 & 124 This is a 1972 Rolls Royce Silver Shadow. This vehicle was heavily armoured and was used for transporting VIPs around London. The car carries the numberplate 'A 210' which was one of the first two index numbers issued to the MPS in 1903. This car remained in service until 2006 and was normally used to transport the Turkish Ambassador. The boot is filled with the radio equipment and the air conditioning unit (because the windows cannot be opened).

125 Rover P6 3500, photographed *c.*1972.

126 This is the Rover P6, Mark 1. This was used extensively by the Metropolitan Police Service around 1972 when this shot was taken.

127 Rover P6 2000 TC, one of only two of this type of car owned by the Metropolitan Police. They were issued to Marylebone and Paddington only, as the area car. This photograph was taken in 1972 and shows the Marylebone car. This model was later replaced by another Rover model with a smaller engine.

128 Rover 3500 P6 Mark 2, area car in zircon blue. The photograph was taken near Victoria in 1972.

129 This is a 1972 Austin 1100 panda car on patrol in a residential area. This was the Met's second panda car model, a successor to the iconic Morris 1000 which had been introduced in 1969. The Austin was introduced in 1972 and was the panda car for around five years.

130 This is a 1972 Austin Cambridge, based at Barnes Traffic Garage. This was used for vehicle removals: officers were equipped with skeleton keys which could open all makes and models of car so they could break in and drive the cars away.

131   Rover P6 and a Triumph motorcycle in a Metropolitan Police workshop in 1976.

132 This is a Rover P6, stationed on the A3 near Claygate in 1973.

133 Land Rover Series 2, Triumph motorcycle, and a Rover 3500 V8 attending the scene of an accident in 1973.

134 1974 Rover P6 3500 area car based at Heathrow airport. All the other area cars of this model were in zircon blue; this was the only white vehicle.

135 Mechanics working on a Triumph 2000 TC at MRD (Main Repair Depot) in Northolt. This was one of several garages at which traffic cars were based and maintenance carried out. This photograph was taken *c.*1971.

136   Stationary Ford Escort 1.1L panda car in 1976.

137 Ford Escort 1.1L panda car in action in 1976.

138 The car is an Austin which was used by senior officers and is beside a Transit with bodywork built by GC Smith Coachbuilders. This was the last of the observation vans that had a cupola built in. The buses are Bedford TK chassis with Maxeta bodywork. The motorcycle is a Triumph. The image was taken in 1979 on North Carriage Drive in Hyde Park, close to Marble Arch.

139-42 This is the Rover 2600 SD1, one of the first production traffic cars. The car is fitted with a Bosch electric two-tone siren under the front bumper. The photographs were taken in 1978 in and around Roehampton and Putney.

143 1985 Land Rover 90 3.5 V-8
4x4. This was used for traffic patrols
and based at Euston Traffic Garage.

144   1985 Land Rover 90 3.5 V-8 4x4. Rear view.

145   1985 Land Rover 110 (phase II) 2.5 V-4 and 1983 Land Rover 110 (phase I) 2.5 V-4. Both these vehicles are fitted with stem lights that can be extended for greater visibility.

146 & 147 1986 Vauxhall Senator 3.0i: this was a traffic car, the only one of this model ever owned by the Metropolitan Police. This vehicle was deployed on the M1, when the Met policed up to Junction 7.

148 & 149   This is a 1987 Ford Granada 2.8iL: another experimental traffic car used by the Metropolitan Police to patrol the M1.

150-2 1987 Land Rover 110 3.5 V-8 with Glover Webb armoured bodywork. This was used by the Territorial Support Group Public Order Unit and was introduced as a direct result of the Brixton Riots of 1985. The vehicles are fully armoured and cost in excess of £100,000 each. The Metropolitan Police had 26 of them as they were deployed in groups of four to the scenes of any trouble. These vehicles were taken out of service in 2006.

153 & 154 1986 Vauxhall Cavalier 1.8L. Traffic car, built specifically for the Metropolitan Police Service.

155 A 1990 Ford Sierra Sapphire 2.0i. This is a Diplomatic Protection Group car, with red livery. The photograph is taken outside the DPG base in Knightsbridge. The DPG first started using red vehicles in 1974 with the Austin 1800 (nicknamed the 'Landcrab'), in order to make DPG cars easily identifiable by embassy security staff.

156-9   1991 Leyland DAF Sherpa 400 3.5 V-8 with armoured bodywork by MacNeillie. These were used as 'Ranger 500' patrols around London for armed robbery and counter terrorism, performing a similar function to the car-based Armed Response Vehicles which were introduced in 1990. These Sherpas remained in service until 2005.

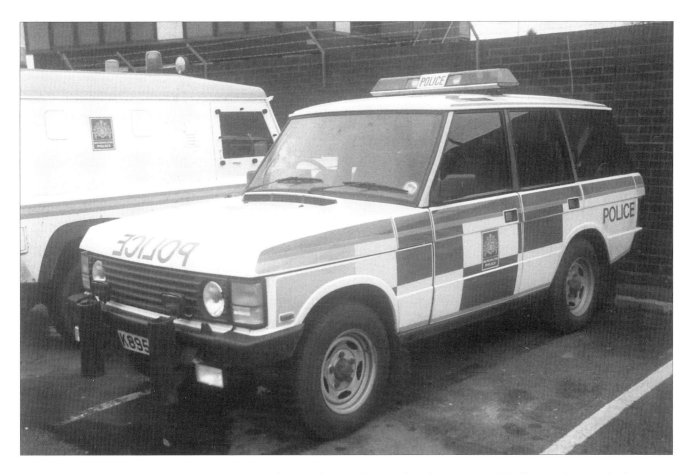

160 & 161　1993 Range Rover Vogue SE 3.9Efi 4x4. This was deployed in the Motorway Traffic Patrol Unit, the first Met Range Rover to bear the Battenberg livery.

162-4 1994 Porsche 968 Club Sport which was used for speed enforcement on the M4. The MPS had only two drivers for this car, who were specially trained by Porsche.

165 & 166   1994 Rover 827Sli traffic patrol car. This was the first Metropolitan Police Car to bear the Battenberg livery which was used experimentally in 1994 and then abandoned until 1996 when it became a national requirement for motorway patrols.

167 & 168   1995 BMW M3, used for motorway speed enforcement. This is an unusual yellow car – BMW only produced this model in black, red and yellow. When the MPS wished to change the colour to white, BMW threatened to withdraw the warranty so it remained yellow. The photograph was taken at Heston services on the M4.

169 & 170   1995 Range Rover II Vogue HSE 4.6 V-8 4x4. This was used on evaluation for motorway patrols.

171 & 172   1996 Land Rover Discovery 2.5tdi 4x4. This is the first car model that the MPS owned and is the duty officer's vehicle at Heathrow (the roof is red to bring the vehicle in line with airport regulations).

173 & 174   This is a 1996 Volvo 850 T-5 Estate. The vehicle was deployed on the M11 for motorway patrols. Volvos were gradually phased out of the Metropolitan Police fleet, to be replaced by BMWs in 1999. 'Battenberg' car markers were introduced in 1990 by Thames Valley Police and were coloured blue, silver and orange at first. The Metropolitan Police did not use Battenberg until it became an ACPO requirement for motorway patrols in 1996. Unlike the other police services in the UK, the majority of the Metropolitan Police fleet is still liveried with the 'jam sandwich' stripes rather than fully marked Battenberg checks.

175 & 176 1996 Volkswagen Golf VR6. This was a Traffic car that was used on evaluation before being deployed as the standard area car in many parts of London. The Golf was not large enough to carry all the kit required in Traffic cars.

177 1999 Ford Focus 1.6. This is one of only two Ford Focuses in the Metropolitan Police Service at the time. The photograph was taken in the yard of the Diplomatic Protection Group behind Kensington High Street.

178 This is a BMW 530D E58, pictured in 2002. This is a design model and the very first BMW that the Metropolitan Police used for an Armed Response Vehicle (ARV).

179-81 2002 BMW 530 Tdi Armed Response Vehicle. This was one of the first MPS cars to carry the new silver livery, since adopted across the MPS fleet. The change to a silver livery was part of a 'spend to save' policy introduced in 2001: silver cars have a higher resale value than white ones. Additionally, silver paint does less environmental damage than white paint.

180 & 181   2002 BMW 530 Tdi Armed Response Vehicle.

Weird and Wonderful

182   This is a 1984 Ford Transit 180 with GC Smith conversion body-work. This was the Metropolitan Police's original bomb disposal vehicle, equipped with a robot in the rear which was deployed to defuse bombs and suspect devices. The vehicle was used regularly during the IRA bombing campaign of mainland UK.

183 & 184 This is a 1979 Ford Transit 180 3.0i V-6, known as 'Pixies'. These were prisoner transport and were hastily adapted to remove the inhabitants of the Libyan Embassy Siege once the drama was over. The rear window was painted out to conceal identities from the waiting press as the survivors of the siege were taken to Sunningdales for after care. Normally used for transporting prisoners, the blue lights and sirens were added for the Libyan Embassy job.

185   1979 Bedford TK Bus Chassis with Maxeta bodywork. This is a major incident bus/control unit, used at Heathrow until 1996.

186-8   This is a 1979 Range Rover 3.5 V-8 4x4, the first Range Rover that the Metropolitan Police used for traffic patrols. They were deployed to patrol the M4. The central blue light was raised (as shown) to a height of five metres but the car could not be moved when the light was deployed as it would bend.

189 & 190   1979 Range Rover 3.5 V-8 4x4, with central blue light lowered.

191-3 These photographs show three models of a fleet of Bedford TK1750s with Locomotors bodywork. This was one of the last of the police's prison vans as the work of prisoner movement was privatised in 1993 (when this photograph was taken). This van has capacity for fourteen prisoners.

192 & 193   1984 Bedford TK1750s with Locomotors bodywork.

194 & 195   This is a Dodge 50 Series with York Engineering trailorwork. This vehicle is a mobile catering unit from 1984. Similar vehicles are in use today, affectionately known as 'Teapot 1' and 'Teapot 2'. These mobile units are on call 24 hours a day to attend police incidents and provide refreshments for the emergency workers at the scene.

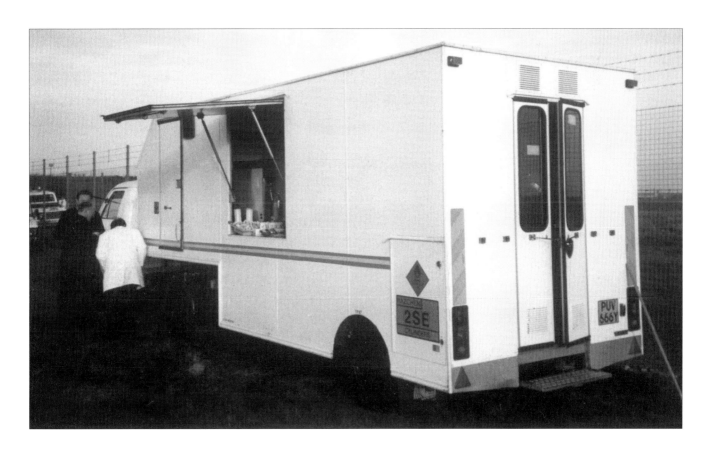

196 & 197   This is a 1984 Bedford TK 4x2 tractor with GC Smith trailer: mobile police station with serving hatches on each side. This photograph was taken outside Harrods.

198 & 199 This is 'Jumbo' – a JCB with armoured bodywork. This is used to remove burning barricades or cars at serious public order operations. 'Jumbo' can lift up to two tonnes and is still in service today.

200 This is a 1990 Talbot Express 6 x 2 chassis with a Rapidex X-ray. This is a mobile X-ray machine for scanning bags at conferences and other high profile events. The MPS still has similar vehicles for deployment nationwide.

201 & 202 This is a 1994 Land Rover 130 2.5tdi pickup. This vehicle was fitted out by Kinetic Special Engineering, with a Hiab Crane to act as a bomb disposal unit. The vehicle is equipped with 800kg of plastic explosives and a length of fire hose. The vehicle, which is remote-controlled, can be driven to a suspected car bomb. The crane is then operated to surround the suspected device with explosive and then a cordon of fire hose, perforated with holes. Once connected to a fire hydrant, this hose would create a wall of water which would enclose the blast. This vehicle was developed in Northern Ireland.

203 & 204   This is a 1998 Iveco Eurocargo 24TE280 with Lambourne Bodywork. This horsebox carries eight horses and also has accommodation for the riders and crew, including a shower facility. This vehicle remains in service today, one of seven owned by the Metropolitan Police. These horseboxes are used for transporting Mounted Branch to the scene of incidents, football matches and other public order events.

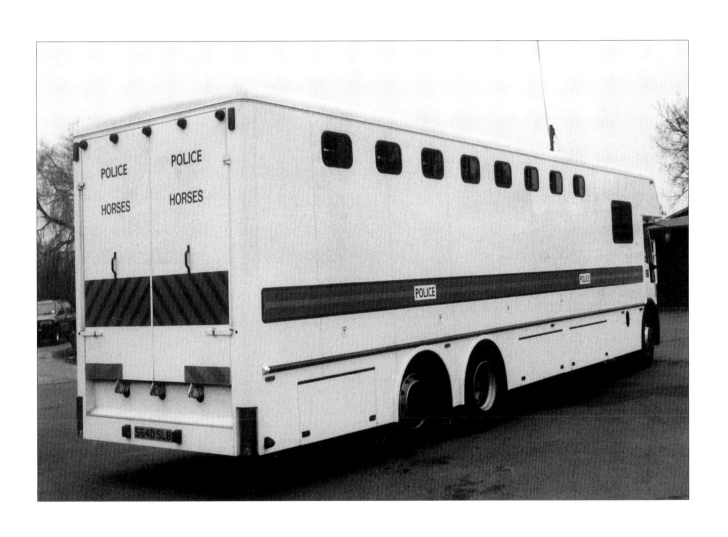

Index